gallery

a collection of pictures and words

Howard Richard Debs

The span from beginning to end is made from all that lies between

Scarlet Leaf Publishing
2017

SCARLET LEAF PUBLISHING HOUSE
TORONTO ONTARIO CANADA

Copyright © 2017 by Howard Richard Debs

ISBN: 978-1-988827-36-0

All rights reserved.

No part of this book can be used or reproduced in any manner whatsoever without written permission, except in the case of brief quotations embodied in critical articles and reviews.

For information address:

Scarlet Leaf Publishing:
scarletleafpublishinghouse@gmail.com

Book Design: Marian Bucataru, darth_valar@zoho.eu

Cover photo by author taken August, 2007. Window washer, Rock 'n' Roll Hall of Fame, Cleveland, Ohio.

All photos in the book are by the author unless otherwise credited. For notes and reflections regarding this and the other images included as well as supplemental material related to the work in general please visit the author's website:
https://howarddebs.com/

Acknowledgments

"Scraps Of Time", "The Butterfly Effect", and "Carrion" appeared previously in *Remarkable Doorways Literary Magazine*

"The Yankee Diner" appeared previously in *Jewish Currents*

"Watching The Moon Rising" appeared previously in *Belle Rêve Literary Journal*

"The Changing Face Of Beauty" appeared previously in *Yellow Chair Review*

"The Concert" appeared previously in *Crack The Spine*

"Kindred Spirits" appeared previously in *Calliope*

"The Cynic", "Sadness In The Midst Of It All", and "Morning Blessings" appeared previously in *InkStain Press*

"There Are No Ghosts In Savannah" appeared previously in *China Grove*

"Being At The Right Place At The Right Time" appeared previously in *Dime Show Review*

"That's Why They Call It The Blues" appeared previously in *Sediments Literary-Arts Journal*

"The Watch in the Pawnshop" and "Blessed Union" appeared previously in *Indiana Voice Journal*

"Body Parts" appeared previously in *Misfitmagazine*

"The Pope's Prayer" and "Repairing The World" appeared previously in *Verse-Virtual*

"Ferguson-Rashomon" appeared previously in *Dissident Voice*

"It's A Biblical Matter", "Learning Right From Wrong", and "Unscathed" appeared previously in *The Basil O'Flaherty*

"The Poetry of Bearing Witness" appeared previously in *On Being On the Blog*

"Terezin: Trilogy Of Names" — "The Walk To Terezin", "The Train To

Terezin", and "The Suitcase To Terezin" appeared previously in *China Grove* and *On Being On the Blog*

"The Tree Of Life" appeared previously in *Poetica Magazine Anna Davidson Rosenberg Poetry Award Collection 2014-2015 Winning Poems*

"A More Perfect Union", "The Dead In Me—A Dirge", "Visitation", "Awakening", and "Dear Daughter Mine" appeared previously in *Scarlet Leaf Review*

"From Generation To Generation" appeared previously in *Dialogual*

"Undercover", "My Friend Is Leaving", and "Sliver Of A Moon" appeared previously in *Clear Poetry Magazine*

"Michael The Wretch" and "Fading Away" appeared previously in *Syzygy Poetry Journal*

"Payday Lender Customer Briefly Seen On TV" appeared previously in *Social Justice Poetry*

"A Virtual Cry For Help" and "Nigeria Is Not Known For Its Scrabble But It Should Be" appeared previously in *I Am Not A Silent Poet*

"I Don't Look Up At The Sky Anymore" and "The Ride: Memoriam For Robin Williams" appeared previously in *Blue Bonnet Review*

"On The Road To Matrimony" appeared previously in *Silver Birch Press*

"Running Out Of Gas" appeared previously in *Star 82 Review*

"Sunrise On Big Pine Key Revisited" Author's note: This recollection invokes the spirit and some words of another poem written after the related experience titled "Sunrise On Big Pine Key" appearing previously in *Belle Rêve Literary Journal*

"Windows, Doors, And Walls" appeared previously in *Poetry Life and Times*

"The New Cat" appeared previously in *The Lake*

"Growing Up With M&M's" appeared previously in *The Galway Review*

Contents

East Gallery — Elsewhere

Scraps Of Time	10
The Yankee Diner	11
Watching The Moon Rising	12
The Butterfly Effect	13
The Changing Face Of Beauty	14
The Concert	15
Kindred Spirits	16
The Cynic	17
There Are No Ghosts In Savannah	18
Being At The Right Place At The Right Time	20
That's Why They Call It The Blues	21
The Watch In The Pawnshop	22

West Gallery — Anywhere

Body Parts	30
The Pope's Prayer	31
Repairing The World	32
Ferguson-Rashomon	33
Carrion	34
Nigeria Is Not Known For Its Scrabble But It Should Be	35
It's A Biblical Matter	36
The Poetry Of Bearing Witness	37
Terezin: Trilogy Of Names —	41
— The Walk To Terezin	41
— The Train To Terezin	43
— The Suitcase To Terezin	45
The Tree Of Life	46

North Gallery — Nowhere

Sadness In The Midst Of It All	48
Undercover	49
Michael The Wretch	50
Payday Lender Customer Briefly Seen On TV	51
A Virtual Cry For Help	53
The Dead In Me—A Dirge	54
The Ride: Memoriam For Robin Williams	55
Visitation	56
Awakening	57
Sliver Of A Moon	58

South Gallery — Somewhere

A More Perfect Union: Excerpts From A Summer Journal	60
From Generation To Generation	62
I Don't Look Up At The Sky Anymore	63
Dear Daughter Mine	64
On The Road To Matrimony	66
The New Cat	67
Growing Up With M&M's	68
Learning Right From Wrong	69
Blessed Union	71
My Friend Is Leaving	73
Unscathed	74
Fading Away	75
Sunrise On Big Pine Key Revisited	76
Running Out Of Gas	78
Morning Blessings	79
Windows, Doors, And Walls	80

A personal note

Gallery is an exhibition to explore life's journey and its encounters of all kinds along the way. Thank you for spending time here.

This volume is dedicated to my wife Sheila, who has given me everything that matters.

East Gallery — Elsewhere

Scraps Of Time

Within the day:
the rush to catch the train
heading downtown running to the office,
jumping into the elevator just seconds
before the closing door to the ninth floor
slipping into the cubicle turning on the
computer, staring at the screen, punching
the keyboard keys answering a stream of
email, time for lunch, down the block,
a fast food line moving never fast enough,
waiting to pay to play the game of life
today, redemption is but a dream.

Within the dream:
standing there, hair blowing
all about in a gentle breeze, the sky is
azure blue, wisps of the whitest clouds
move slowly across our view
we wait, no need to rush,
we sit on a stump as day turns to dusk;
we stay to hear the whippoorwill call,
its song ethereal in the distance,
as the day's departing rays send spears
of light through the forest trees we recall
legend has it this bird can save our soul.

The Yankee Diner

Real food
on the grill
bacon grease
laced slice of
apple pie hot
bubbling apple
juice spilling down
the sides of the
deep browned crust
percolating on the
sturdy ordinary
crockery dish
no fine china this
is the real deal
it's all inside
see the gilt edged
chrome shine red
Naugahyde
stools soldiered up
along the Formica
counter hear the
short order patois:
short stack two
over easy
hash browns
slathered and
smothered
blue plate
special
meatloaf
platter BLT
hold the mayo.
Real people
blue collar
white collar
open collar tee
shirt undershirt
baggy pants
blue jeans
short shorts tie
dye baseball
caps police
officers' hats
all there.
Real life
laughing rowdy
angry tears let
her alone no
more fights get
your own don't
walk away on
me keep the
ring he doesn't
care it doesn't
matter it's too
late got to go
work you know
call me later
it hurt big-time
never again
big game this
weekend why
didn't she tell
you who knew
it won't happen
promise never
mind can't you find
the time?
Real time
on their way to the
bus to visit a sick
aunt going to the
lawyer to sign the
divorce papers
heading uptown for
a job interview
taking the kids to
see granny at the
nursing home
rushing for class
one more day all
alone a cup of joe
and one more to go
the night watchman
leaves paying for his
breakfast telling the
waitress to keep
the change.

Watching The Moon Rising

Watching the moon rising,
reclaim your sense of place in our world.
The hoary Hebrew calendar counts the moon,
Stonehenge watches for the sun.
It all comes down to us from ancient celestial mysteries
and still we are enthralled by these mystical memories.

When you rise up, the sun is in the east
and when you lie down, the sun is west
and going down somewhere in tune
with its universal rhythm
while the moon is rising in its own time
and if you are down in a valley
you can stand, lifting your head, looking upward
watching the moon rising
over the hills in the distance, far away
and if the full moon is rising
in all its grandeur you can feel your place on earth,
a small still voice within this sphere.

While your feet may yet be planted firmly on the ground,
but gazing up toward the firmament your eyes
are mesmerized by the giant orb of night,
now you can consider your destiny, and the way you will go
following the sun? Rising with the moon?

The wolf howls at the moon,
we humans wonder,
watching the moon rising.

The Butterfly Effect

"It's impossible for humans to measure everything infinitely accurately."
—Robert Devaney, mathematics professor, Boston University

It was an ordinary day, whatever that means.
It starts out that way, but it doesn't always
stay that way because along the way things
happen to make it another kind of day
than you think it will be or could be
but it might not end up that way either
because there is no known reason for some
things turning out the way they do sometimes
which is to say you just don't
always know what will happen.

You look for the ultimate answer, the final absolute
no doubt about it unalterable answer the one thing
it most certainly must be but then you realize it
might be some other unforeseen unexpected thing
that just happens without you noticing at all and
in the process completely alters an ordinary day.

A Monarch butterfly stretches its wings to the sun,
just to bask in the warmth of the day,
while bound south for Mexico
and that might change the velocity
of the surrounding air in such a way
to produce in its train a chain of events
that bring about a massive storm somewhere in
Chile, or Honduras, or Ecuador or elsewhere
in the Western Hemisphere but no one would
know the cause was the butterfly. . . .

He waits in the corridor,
outside the hospital
room where his brother
was just told the
diagnosis. It is a rare form
of cancer. It is terminal —
The butterfly?

The Changing Face Of Beauty

The Japanese have made an art of it, golden repair
—after a commentary on Kintsugi, lacquerware mending

Soon these,
as with the picture of
Dorian Gray, will bear wilted
petals golden hues succumbing
becoming burnt umber
taking on another cast,
reflecting not the past
but the passage of time.

***

Long ago in what too will change
from a quaint fishing village
called Edo to a burgeoning Tokyo
a craftsman ponders a conundrum
in his ceramics shop one spring day,
looking towards a sky of periwinkle blue
he searches the heavens for an answer
amidst that exquisite view
the delicate porcelain masterpiece
known as "two flowers" fragile as
its namesake sits upon his bench
then, after examining each crack,
each spidery wrinkle
conceded from use,
with care he fills
the fissures
applying a lacquer
and metallic mix
the object of his art
now showing its wear
in shimmering
golden seams
not hiding what
came to be—
redeeming
the changing
face of beauty.

The Concert

I.

This is news as
much as anything.
Carnegie Hall will
be hosting the
return from the dead
of the viola da gamba
a mainstay of Baroque.
On Monday April 13
the seats in
this august place
will be filled with
Early Music supporters
there to hear vibrant
echoes of the past.
They will be
transplanted back
in time to a simpler time
when—

II.

"Milord methinks
the musicians are
ready to commence
The concert," listen:
the plaintive
undulations of strings
of gut calling out
a woeful and mournful
sigh, appealing to the heart
and soul. The horsehair bow
stroking the strings like a lover
the audience completely hushed
In order to hear the tremulous
rush of notes outpouring from the
front of the hall, reverberating
off the wall, caressing all in
harmony with the ebb and flow
of one's very own blood coursing
through one's own veins; the pulse of the music
emulating a rhythm akin to the rapture in
life itself.

Kindred Spirits

There is a magic mirror
somewhere in the world
and if you find it
when you look into it
you can see others like you
in your reflection—

So a man walks into a bar
and sits on a stool at the end
and orders a gin to begin.
Then another arrives
sits down by his side
and calls for a gin as well.

The strangers start to speak:
Where might you be from, one says.
A small town called Sleepy Holler
you prob'ly never heard of it.
Well I'll be, says the other,
My grandfather lived in Peekin,
just down the road from there.
He worked a farm there all his life, I used
to go for visits, he taught me how to fly fish, do you?
Sure do, his barmate replied. Nothin' like fly fishin'!
A man and his thoughts and fish, nothin' better, said he.
What brings you to town this soggy night then? he asks.
I've got a horse to show at the Weir County Fair.
No really? Same for me, came the reply.
Barkeep, another round; make it gin agen
for me and my friend.

—So you see
what can be.
We are not alone.

The Cynic

I'm a hundred
and one
I've seen
everything
that can be done,
here in Beantown
where I come from.
Talk about your
son of a bitch politicians
there's a line
as long as your arm.
Curley goin' back to the 30s,
White who ran against
Louise Hicks back in '67,
or was that '66? A woman
ain't no different.
My old pa used to say
if things keep goin' this way
they'll run out of candidates
one fine day!
Will Rogers had it right,
he said somethin' like
if you put truth into
politics you'd have
no politics.
Now they've sure got a
lot this time around;
it's a great pissin' contest
that's for sure
but we're the real
losers as usual
sucker punched by a
bunch of sneaky petes.
It don't matter if you're
Democrat, Republican, or
Independent, all politicians
are just plain crooked.

There Are No Ghosts in Savannah

It started out an ordinary summer day. Sticky hot. He sat that morning in the usual way, at Clary's Café nearby the more than 150 year old Forsyth Park with its "Fragrant Garden for the Blind", for whom there are name plaques in Braille for such things unseen, as well an 1879 Confederate War Memorial, and a stunning fountain modeled after ones at Place de la Concorde in Paris. He watched the others partake of their Lowcountry breakfast fare, hot buttered grits, corned beef hash, Clary's own scrambled egg concoction, hoppel poppel. Sitting alfresco under an awning, he knew he could hear the sounds from the grand fountain in the park a few blocks away, the water spray splashing from heralding stone Tritons forming rivulets in the fountain's pool basin full with wishing well superstition. He arrived downtown at Colonial Park by half past noon to pay his respects as always. The Old Brick Graveyard as it was formerly called was founded in 1750, second oldest in the city, closed to further internments in 1853, declared a park. He took the northern entrance on Abercorn Street passing under the watchful eye of the bronze eagle perched atop the Georgia granite arching gate erected there in 1913 by the local chapter of the Daughters of the American Revolution bearing the engraved letters D.A.R. some say pronounced as a word as "dare". They say 10,000 are buried there. They say it is considered to be one of the most haunted cemeteries in all of Savannah.

They say that beneath Savannah lay old tunnels where victims of the 1876 Yellow Fever epidemic were buried to stave off panic at the sight of so many dead. There are tunnels leading to the river some say, pirates' tunnels, tunnels of the Underground Railroad that snake throughout the city as well. Who would dare go there? Now Savannah has had for years a Voodoo culture. Legends abound about how in Voodoo it is possible to raise the dead. Before Colonial Park Cemetery was closed at night it was told that morning visitors would find remnants of a Voodoo ceremony performed the night before. Bones and disturbed earth found around graves. Of the number of plots where he paused on this occasion, he stopped and stood mulling over the gravestone epitaph of one particularly, as many times he had before, it reads in part:

> *James Wilde, Esquire*
> *He fell in a duel on the 16th of January, 1815, by the hand of a man who, a short time ago, would have been friendless but for him. . . . By his untimely death the prop of a Mother's age is broken: The hope and consolation of Sisters is destroyed, the pride of Brothers humbled in the dust and a whole family, happy until then, overwhelmed with affliction.*

Wilde, a Lieutenant, 8th Regiment, U.S. Infantry had served in the campaign against the Seminoles in Florida. Richard Henry Wilde, the poet and U.S. Representative was the young officer's brother. It is said the vivid stories the soldier brother told, inspired the poet brother to pen an epic poem, never finished, cut short as was his brother's life. Here, the opening stanza, it reads in part:

> *My life is like the summer rose,*
> *That opens to the morning sky,*
> *But, ere the shades of evening close,*
> *Is scattered on the ground – to die!*

As night came to shroud the city over at the Owens-Thomas house which in its nadir succumbed to the status of a boarding house where its most famous guest, the French General Marquis de Lafayette, a true Revolutionary War hero, during a visit in 1825 addressed a crowd of hundreds from the ornate veranda on the south façade of the mansion, there was a report a group of visitors on a private tour had witnessed the visage of a human form dressed in U.S. Infantry officer's uniform, staring at them in the dining room down the long hall, then disappearing, walking through a wall. There are no ghosts in Savannah—but only during daylight.

Being At The Right Place At The Right Time

I went to Indonesia to see the total eclipse of the sun, the only one in 2016. I planned carefully, for while its path is counted in hours across the globe, it can be seen in its totality for mere minutes at best.

I went with a friend. We decided to parlay our chances for success so he went to Palembang, a very large city in Sumatra, I took myself to Bali.

The chance for a full eclipse itself is rare. Everything has to be just right. My friend texted me from the city's landmark Ampera bridge where thousands had gathered, old men who wanted one more look before their passing, mothers carrying their babies, "we cannot see from here, too cloudy, but the darkness somehow moves us all no less."

The day of the eclipse in the Balinese calendar fell on a holiday devoted to silence. Permission was given allowing for special prayer services during this cosmic event. The praying did not succeed. Bali, thought a paradise by some was not to be that for me, as I did not see what I came to see. I did see the birds go amok, confused by dark falling again after dawn.

That's Why They Call It The Blues

Today we got the news
Magic Slim died, the last of a triad.
First there was Muddy, then Howlin' Wolf
now Slim, he's left, took his guitar licks too.
A procession of Deep South musicians
from the sorry back roads and bayous
of Mississippi, Tennessee, Louisiana
kept on comin' up to Chi-town
and electrified the blues on Maxwell
Street and on Chicago's South Side
where the forebears of rock 'n' roll
paid their dues in the honkytonks and dives.
Get a sound of your own they said,
and he did. Magic Slim and the Teardrops.
Raining down today, teardrops for
the groove that's gone away.
Play the Alligator, Rooster, Chess records,
if you can find them, watch the vinyl spinning
on a turntable relic if you can find one
hear the cries of pain, hard luck,
hard times, the blues seventh chords,
the mic'd up harmonica wail
that's why they call it the blues—Coda:

Down on your luck blues,
Pinch a penny blues,
Bill collector knockin'
at the door blues,
Water and stale bread blues,
Sleepin' in the gutter blues,
Got those only the clothes
on your back blues,
The coughin' up blood blues,
The hound dogs a-comin' after you blues,
The judge ain't kind blues
Walkin' round the prison yard blues
Got a feelin' I'm never
gonna make it outta
here alive blues.

The Watch in the Pawnshop

It was that time of the month. He was due. He didn't have the money he hoped to set aside to pay to ransom his previously pawned belongings, his grandfather's bejeweled necktie stickpin, a gold religious medallion given to him by his wife which he had worn around his neck throughout the war, and another family heirloom, a ring with an amethyst stone, sizable and deep purple, "good quality," the pawnbroker had admitted, "worth at least a few bucks." He would have to pay the interest, keep the loan going, hold out for another month. But how?

He needed a job after coming home from fighting in the Pacific, just like all the others returning from World War II. So he used his muster out pay and was able to obtain a hack license. After all, he had a family to feed. His wife gave birth to a baby boy, 7 pounds 8 ounces, all 23 inches of him, while he was overseas. Somehow he got a picture which came one day in the mail call. He was proud as all get out. He took the picture around to his buddies, "I've got a son," he boasted.

It wasn't exactly like he thought it would be. Pats on the back don't pay the bills. So he drove a cab. It was an honest living, but it hardly made ends meet once the rent was paid, and the groceries bought,

22

the electric taken care of, and this past month, a new dress for Sarah, his wife. She hadn't had anything new for quite some time. He wanted to do this for her, so he hocked his stuff, and now he was paying the piper.

He parked his cab outside the Canal Street Pawnshop at Canal and Eldridge Streets on the Lower East Side. He was looking for Ernie, but Ernie was out to lunch. He was stuck with Ernie's boss. "Hey, I'm due tomorrow. I don't have it. How'd this be?" He took a photo out of a manila envelope.

"My buddy was one of the marines that hoisted the flag on Iwo Jima. He gave me this picture and signed it, too. It's gotta be worth what I owe ya."

"Look pal, how do I know who signed this photo. You need cash on the barrelhead, my friend. You got 24 hours, now scram."

Dejected, he walked along Canal Street to the Cup & Saucer diner he frequented, and went inside. He sat at the counter.

"Hey Gladys, can I get a cup of joe?

"Sure, you look pretty blue, what's wrong, honey?"

"I need some green, I'm kinda in a jam."

"Here's your coffee, on the house. Just keep pluggin' away, you'll figure it out."

"Thanks, I owe you big time, sweetheart."

He went back, started his cab and began cruising the streets looking for a fare. He had his share that night. Actually it was better than he had expected. At the end of his shift, he went to clean out the back of his cab. Somebody had left the Daily News on the floor and he found an empty Camel cigarette pack crumpled in the corner of the back seat and right by the door he saw it. A pocket watch. It was gold for sure. One of his fares left it behind no doubt, maybe it fell out of a pocket or a purse when the passenger went to pay. He knew he should tell the cab company and turn it over.

Someone would be calling and asking if it had been found. But he needed that watch. It was his ticket to get his stuff out of hock. He didn't think twice. He thought to himself, *it was meant to be.*

◊

The notice appeared in the New York Times Lost and Found classified ads within days:

> *Lost — Gold pocket watch, unusual design, in Lower Manhattan. Finder please return and receive liberal reward. Return to Hotel Astor.*

Clem Darling was head of the city's pawnbrokers' association. It was nearly 6 a.m. He was on his way out to breakfast after a rough night. He had his hands full the night before. A knife fight, a stolen painting, and a bunch of counterfeit bills, just for starters. He loved to read, fiction, poetry, you name it, and he was great with words. He remembered "hock" was from the Dutch, meaning a miserable place like a pen, a sty, a prison. As he headed towards the door to his office, thinking of bacon and eggs, he heard the phone ring again. He wasn't going to answer, and then relented. Some hockshop needs my help, he thought.

"Mr. Darling, this is Detective King, from the 9th Precinct. I don't normally get involved in this kind of thing, but the higher-ups asked me to handle this one personally. You get my drift? We're looking for some lost or stolen property. It's a watch. A gold pocket watch. It's actually pretty special. You can tell time in the dark with it. I want you to see if that watch is in one of your pawnshops?"

"Who's the rightful owner, can you say?"

"I'm afraid I can't divulge that information, Darling. Just give us a hand here, we cover for you all the time, now it's your turn."

"No problem, I'll ask around and get back to you right away."

He started making calls. He knew what was at stake. The police were the lynchpin in the pawnshop world. Like the bird that picks bugs off a bull gets a free ride and protection as its reward. A cop on the beat had dropped off a detailed description of the watch sent over from Detective King. So far, he had phoned about twelve pawnshops and nobody remembered anybody bringing in such a watch. He decided to send around a flyer to some of the pawnshops in the area involved by courier. A day later, he got the call.

"I'm lookin' at the watch you're after, Clem." It was Ernie from the Canal Street Pawnshop.

"Is it in good shape?"

"Perfect, not a scratch. Now what do we do? I'm out a bundle."

"There's a pretty good reward involved, I think. That should make it right."

"What about the customer information, how do you want to deal with it?"

"We've got to turn everything over as usual, that's that."

◊

He sat in the police station interrogation room, cold sweat beading on his brow. His hands were shaking. He kept thinking he should have turned over that damned watch in the first place. He got his stuff back alright, Ernie at the pawnshop snatched up the watch like it was one of the keys to the kingdom. "Never seen anything quite like this" was what Ernie said, he didn't ask any questions. But Detective King asked questions.

"I'll ask this just one time, and I expect the truth. Did you swipe that watch?" The detective had steely eyes that pierced right through the taxi driver's gut when he asked this.

"I didn't steal anything. OK, I found it in my cab after I finished for the night. I should have brought it around to the cab company. I used it to redeem a pawnshop loan. I had some family stuff I hocked, that stuff meant a lot to me. Look, I let my emotions get the best of me, I admit it. It was wrong. Now what's gonna happen, whatcha gonna do with me?"

"You lucky bastard, nothing is going to happen to you. The owner isn't going to press charges. Now get the hell out of here and keep your ass out of trouble, you hear me!"

◊

Charlie, the dispatcher at the cab company called him over as soon as he came into the garage.

"Get over here I've got something important for you to do."

"What's up Charlie, I start my shift pretty soon."

"It'll have to wait. You're to go to the Hotel Astor for a pickup and delivery. It's all in this note. Don't screw up, this is V.I.P. stuff."

He left his cab at the cab stand outside the hotel, walked into the lobby and presented the note from Charlie to the front desk clerk. "Just a moment," said the clerk. He picked up the house phone and made a call. "Go on up, room 1102, the elevator's around the corner, take it to the top floor."

He got off the elevator on the 11th floor and walked down the hall until he found the right room number. He knocked on the door. The door opened and an older woman greeted him. "Come right in, please, she's been expecting you, she wanted to meet you."

They met for half an hour. He explained everything. She let him know she understood. He was immensely relieved and grateful. He had brought the picture of the flag raising on Iwo Jima. He wanted her to have it as a token of his appreciation for not pressing charges against him, it was all he had of value. He told her the copy of the famous photo had been signed by a fellow marine buddy who had been one of the flag raisers. He wasn't sure she'd accept it, but she did and then she asked him to do her a favor. "Anything, just name it," he said in almost a whisper. She handed him a small bound volume and asked him to take it to the office of the head of the pawnbrokers' association in Manhattan.

By the time the taxi driver arrived at Clem Darling's office, it was late in the afternoon. "Here, these are for you." He gave Darling the book he had been given along with a note. It was a thank you note. The book contained a poem of some length, it began:

Come walk with me, and I will tell

What I have read in this scroll of stone;

I will spell out this writing on hill and meadow.

It is a chronicle wrought by praying workmen,

The forefathers of our nation—

Darling thumbed through the pages, back and forth, stopping at the dedication page. He started reading:

When I began The Song of the Stone Wall, Dr. Edward Everett Hale was still among us, and it was my intention to dedicate the poem to him if it should be deemed worthy of publication. I fancied that he would like it; for he loved the old walls and the traditions that cling about them.

As I tried to image the men who had built the walls long ago, it seemed to me that Dr. Hale was the living embodiment of whatever was heroic in the founders of New England. He was a great American. He was also a great Puritan. Was not the zeal of his ancestors upon his lips, and their courage in his heart? Had they not bequeathed to him their torch-like faith, their patient fervor of toil and their creed of equality?

But his bright spirit had inherited no trace of their harshness and gloom. The windows of his soul opened to the sunlight of a joyous faith. His optimism and genial humor inspired gladness and good sense in others. With an old story he prepared their minds to receive new ideas, and with a parable he opened their hearts to generous feelings. All men loved him because he loved them. They knew that his heart was in their happiness, and that his humanity embraced their sorrows. In him the weak found a friend, the unprotected, a champion. Though a herald and proclaimer of peace, he could fight stubbornly and passionately on the side of justice. His was a lovable, uplifting greatness which drew all men near and ever nearer to God and to each other. Like his ancestors, he dreamed of a land of freedom founded on the love of God and the brotherhood of man, a land where each man shall achieve his share of happiness and learn the work of manhood to rule himself and lend a hand.

Thoughts like these were often in my mind as the poem grew and took form. It is fitting, therefore, that I should dedicate it to him, and in so doing I give expression to the love and reverence which I have felt for him ever since he called me his little cousin, more than twenty years ago.

Helen Keller

Wrentham, Massachusetts,

January, 1910.

Author's Notes:

1.   Quoted matter of Helen Keller's The Song of the Stone Wall is in the public domain and taken from the Project Gutenberg eBook version available online at: http://www.gutenberg.org/cache/epub/12093/pg12093.html

2.   Helen Keller's "touch watch", the prized possession on which this short story is based, was temporarily "lost" during a trip to New York in 1952. For further information about this special timepiece visit The Smithsonian web page: http://americanhistory.si.edu/collections/search/object/nmah_851873

3.   Photo credit: Taxis in Manhattan, early 1950s; oldnycphotos.com used with permission.

West Gallery — Anywhere

Body Parts

I just heard the news,
on All Things Considered
so it must be true.

The New York City Medical
Examiner's Office is still,
twelve years after the attacks,
telephoning family members
of victims of the 9/11 tragedy
and informing them that
an upper arm, a leg, a tooth,
has been finally identified
as belonging to their relative,
who died that infamous day.

One mother gets such a notice.
She has buried a son, or those bits of
his remains found in the wreckage.
Now some other physical part
has been positively confirmed through
DNA sampling, or other scientific methods,
modern means unavailable,
for example after Auschwitz, to allow loved ones
access to the pieces of a person.

So what do you say when such
a call comes your way?
Hello, oh thank you, just send it to the cemetery.
There the remains will be exhumed,
the casket opened, placing the upper arm,
the leg, the tooth, inside then to be returned
to the earth. A new burial, a relived agony.
The report says some prefer not to know.
They can request to be noted on a list labeled
"do not call" and the parts in question are removed
to the 9/11 Memorial, to a special holding place
so that in a time to come, if the loved one should
change their mind, they can inquire:
is my brother there, anywhere, any part of him?

The report states, 22,000 individual remains
were recovered. 14,000 individual body parts
belonging to 1,634 people have been identified . . .
to date.

The Pope's Prayer

I read somewhere that in the year 2000
Pope John Paul II, now a saint,
while at the Western Wall on a visit to Israel—following
the custom of most others who
find themselves there—placed a small piece of paper
in a crevice in the Wall on which were written
these words:

*God of our fathers,
You chose Abraham and his descendants
to bring your Name to the Nations:
we are deeply saddened
by the behaviour of those
who in the course of history
have caused these children of yours to suffer,
and asking your forgiveness
we wish to commit ourselves to
genuine brotherhood
with the people of the Covenant.*

I have just discovered that all such notes
as these filled with wishes and prayers by
the thousands are removed each year with care
using wooden sticks dipped in the cleansing
mikveh ritual bath to make room for
the succeeding year's expected messages: the
words of hope, the thoughts of peace,
the requests for health—the scraps of paper
with these pleas will be taken for burial...
It is but fitting that the collective outpouring
of so many from all walks of life—
the pieces of pain, the scraps of yearning,
the writings of rumination, be together—
from dust to dust.

Repairing The World

The end is not yet.
The beginning came before.
We are in the middle.
What do we do within
this space and time?
Are we petrified?
Are we willing?
Are we dumbfounded?
We have a place to start.
It is the beating heart.
Pulsating, coursing with the
message that we are alive.

We can stand, walk,
run, see, feel, smell, speak, hear,
think, we can go on, or
stand still, like a statue,
cold and unmoved.

Feel: the pain of the mother holding her
bloated child dying of hunger in a
wretched refugee camp in Somalia.

Smell: the putrid musty odor
of bodies decomposing in the hell of
a despot's war on his own people in Syria.

Hear: the muffled cries of young girls
forced to do the bidding of their pimps
in the cribs of Thailand.

Speak: to the homeless
huddled under a bridge in America.

From the four corners of the world,
gather our destitute—our disclaimed—
under a canopy of healing.

We can make this better.

Ferguson-Rashomon

For these words alone, I was ready to pardon . . .
—from Rashomon, the movie

In 1950 a Japanese period film
portrayed the killing of a samurai
and the rape of his wife.
Four separate and different
versions of the tragedy are
vividly told by the characters
in the story: the bandit, the wife,
the samurai (as told through
a medium), and the woodcutter.

Who speaks the truth?
Who knows the truth?
Who hides the truth?
What is the truth?

A priest, with whom
the woodcutter shares
his story becomes disillusioned.
He begins to lose his faith
in humanity, seeing
each person
shaping a reality
colored by their
particular interest.
Then the woodcutter
does something magnanimous
restoring the priest's
hope for humankind.

Carrion

Two large black birds
maybe ravens, hard to say,
were seen picking at a carcass
in the road.
Roadkill no doubt,
who can tell?
What was it? A possum,
possibly, a raccoon, hard to know.
Whatever, it must have strayed
onto the roadway and must have
gotten in the way of some
night time driver heading
to Santa Fe, or just going home.
It was after all, a dark night,
a rain had lightly fallen, the
pavement therefore wet and slick,
the car just might have had
a skid, it's tough to be sure
in such cases what really
causes such a poor creature's demise.
There was blood no doubt, blood
all around, it seems not even rain
can wash away the blood of
that which is now defined as—
dead and decaying—carrion.

Nigeria Is Not Known For Its Scrabble But It Should Be

Last November, in the final of the World Scrabble Championship held in Australia, the Nigerian known as "The Cat in the Hat" for his penchant for fedoras beat a Brit becoming headline news in his homeland.

It is now considered that earlier reports incorrectly stated that a schoolgirl/mother rescued from Boko Haram was one of the 276 taken from the town of Chibok in 2014. Another girl also rescued was indeed one of those so abducted.

The strategy of the Nigerians who have the unheralded distinction of having more top 200 Scrabble players than any other country is a short-word approach, eschewing the long-word approach long held to be the sine qua non of the game.

Boko fighters have killed 20,000 since 2009, have kidnapped more than 2000 since 2014, mostly females; in pursuing their maniacal efforts, they have the reprehensible distinction of being ranked as the world's deadliest terror group.

The advent of the Nigerian Scrabble method, known for rack management, a defensive style, pins its success on the unintended consequences of using up all seven tiles each round, and on certain design quirks of the playing board itself, which strangely favor shorter words.

The advent of Boko Haram can be pinned to the Nigerian history of dictatorial regimes, spawning corruption, social inequality, poverty, and horrendous human rights abuses including summary executions, torture, rape, restrictions on freedom of speech, press, assembly, religion, and movement.

The Nigerian Scrabble concept is changing the game. Using computer application simulations and analytics, a secret list exists of the five-letter words that are most difficult for opponents to utilize. Knowledge of the five-letter words can result in beating the seven-, eight-, nine-letter word players. The Wellington Foundation for Scrabble and Mind Development in Africa has lobbied the government to add Scrabble to the national curriculum, success in this undertaking remains in question.

The current Nigerian President was elected last year on a pledge to destroy Boko Haram, and a combination of anti-Boko vigilantes, volunteer locals, and the army have mounted a counterinsurgency campaign to recapture Boko territory village by village,
success in this undertaking is uncertain.

It's a Biblical Matter

Green Beret Who
Beat Up Afghan Officer for
Raping Boy Can Stay in Army
so reads the headline
in *The New York Times*
The Afghan kept the child
chained to a bed as a sex
slave the article notes
"morally we could no longer
stand by and allow the Afghan
local police to commit atrocities"
it is reported the Green Beret
told Army officials
Bacha bāzī literally
"boy play"; is a slang term in
Afghanistan for a wide variety
of activities that involve
child sexual abuse and pederasty
so reads the first sentence in
the Wikipedia article on the topic
The Green Beret was relieved
of his command, he was to be
discharged, there were appeals
to fully reinstate him, *The Times*
article continues, Army policy
instructs American soldiers
not to intervene in cases of child
sex abuse by their Afghan allies
Moses saw an Egyptian beating
A Hebrew . . . He turned this way
and that and, seeing no one about,
he struck down the Egyptian
and hid him in the sand so
reads the verse from Exodus.

The Poetry of Bearing Witness

> *"To write poetry after Auschwitz is barbaric."*
> —*Theodor Adorno*

The Jewish poet since biblical times cannot remain silent. I am a Jewish poet.

For these past 30 years, I have searched for a way to bear witness, a role Elie Wiesel himself urges upon us. In his 2003 Days of Remembrance address at the United States Holocaust Memorial Museum (USHMM), he asked, "Who will bear witness for the witness?"—reminding us of the question posed by poet Paul Celan. A few years earlier in 2001, Elie Wiesel spoke these words:

"How does one mourn for six million people who died? How many candles does one light? How many prayers does one recite? Do we know how to remember the victims, their solitude, their helplessness? They left us without a trace, and we are their trace."

Elie Wiesel gives permission to speak up and to speak for those who cannot speak.

Finally I came upon a possibility. One of my areas of special poetic interest is ekphrastic poetry, a form which takes its inspiration from pictorial and other artwork. Many years ago, I had been privileged to experience "The Precious Legacy" exhibit then touring the United States. It was a selection of artifacts from the remarkable collection of the Jewish Museum in Prague. As it happens, Prague is very close to home, my ancestral home, actually. My paternal grandfather came to America from Riga, Latvia, in 1886.

The exhibition, which toured from 1983 to 1986, gave those who saw it a look at a small part of an extraordinary collection of Judaica. The Museum's treasures exist due to an ironic twist of fate. From 1942 to 1945, the Nazis confiscated Jewish possessions of artistic and historical value throughout Bohemia and Moravia (the Czech Republic), and whilst Jews of these lands were being deported to captivity and death, these artifacts were shipped to Prague. The Nazis' intention was to establish a "museum to an extinct race" that would justify to the world the "final solution to the Jewish question." Prague was spared from wartime destruction, as was the collection of Judaica that by war's end filled more than 50 warehouses throughout the city.

These artifacts were silent witnesses from the time. I could give them a voice, and in this way let them speak for themselves through me—a bold, but plausible mission.

I contacted Jakub Hauser, the curator of the vast photographic collection of the Jewish Museum, and presented my idea. I asked if the museum would grant permission for me to select and use a number of archival photographs from the collection for a series of poetic statements about them, as well as a selection of extant art and writing of children and adult prisoners, principally of the ghetto-camp at Terezin. The museum agreed.

The intent of the work in progress is to explicate and illustrate the indomitable spirit for good juxtaposed by the inevitable potential for evil—what in Hebrew is called *yetzer hatov/yetzer hara*, "good inclination"/"evil inclination."

I chose Terezin as the focus of the work, as the camp has become associated with the spiritual resistance of the Shoah. Thirty-three thousand perished at Terezin. In all, some 140,000 Jews were transferred to Terezin, of which nearly 90,000 were ultimately sent to points further east and to almost certain death. Fifteen thousand children passed through Terezin. Approximately 90 percent of these children perished in death camps.

> *"Still the story had to be told. In spite of all risks, all possible misunderstandings."*
>
> —*Elie Wiesel, "Entre Deux Soleils"*

On a Sunday—April 9, 2000 to be exact—a windy day with almost a record low and light snow falling in the early morning, the United States Holocaust Memorial Museum held a special daylong program devoted to poetry of the Holocaust. The keynote was delivered by the Nobel laureate and poet Czeslaw Milosz. A Catholic turned atheist returned to Catholicism, he was a member of the resistance in Warsaw during World War II. Eighty-nine at the time, Milosz died four years later in 2004. In an interview after his presentation, Milosz stated that the only credible poetic response to the Holocaust is in writing about anything and everything else, perhaps to assert in this way hope in the promise that there can be life after death in a collective sense.

So what of those who dare to "speak" of it?

While there are countless poems, there is hardly a work tackling the why and the what of the genre per se. Can there be and should there be Holocaust poetry? Seven lion and lioness literary luminaries joined the fray in a series of seven articles in the *Michigan Quarterly Review*.

Joy Ladin contends that there isn't, and shouldn't be, a corpus of poetry of and about the Holocaust, only allowing for the attempt of individual poems. Seeming to agree in a sense with Adorno's admonition, Ladin maintains it is, prima facie, impossible to do justice to the experience of the Holocaust—that trying to turn the tragedy into an aesthetic piece of poetry is a travesty, that the experience is inexpressible.

Sandra Gilbert counters:

"It's the poet's task—often the poet's excruciatingly painful task—to testify to pain and grief with all the skill and inspiration he or she can muster."

Wendy Steiner puts it this way:

"The atrocity of the Holocaust lay in part in its elimination of the personal in favor of universals and generalizations... It seems a terrible irony to argue that a Holocaust poem cannot be good if it expresses just a single human sensibility."

Susan Gubar, whose book *Poetry after Auschwitz: Remembering What One Never Knew* on poetry and the Holocaust really started the fracas, makes the case:

"Poetry has a privileged place because it enables its creators and readers to experience... on the one hand, the realization that it cannot be comprehended in its full horror and, on the other hand, the urgency of attempting to comprehend."

But it is Alicia Ostriker who most strongly challenges Ladin's polemic:

"Writing is what poets do about trauma. We try to come to grips with what threatens to make us crazy, by surrounding it with language."

And the coup de grace:

"It has always seemed to me that to fall silent in the aftermath of the Holocaust is to surrender to it. How can one write poetry after Auschwitz? How can one not?"

Quoting Dmitri Shostakovich, she writes, "People knew about Babi Yar before Yevtushenko's poem, but they were silent. Art destroys silence."

So I will continue with my project. I am encouraged by the words of Victor Frankl, psychotherapist and Holocaust survivor, who, in 1946, wrote *Man's Search for Meaning*:

> *"Then I grasped the meaning of the greatest secret that human poetry and human thought and belief have to impart: The salvation of man is through love and in love."*

Leopold Zunz, a German Reform rabbi and writer who is considered the founder of Judaic Studies, wrote in 1855:

> *"If there are ranks in suffering, Israel takes precedence of all the nations; if the duration of sorrows and the patience with which they are borne ennoble, the Jews can challenge the aristocracy of every land; if a literature is called rich in the possession of a few classic tragedies—what shall we say to a National Tragedy lasting for fifteen hundred years, in which the poets and the actors were also the heroes?"*

It is highly unlikely that those who choose to write of and about the Holocaust do so to be considered as heroes. More likely, the purpose is to strike one more match to keep the flame of memory and truth ignited.

Quoted matter from Michigan Quarterly Review used with permission.

From my work in progress, I offer "Terezin: Trilogy Of Names"—

Photo from the archive, Jewish Museum in Prague, used with permission

The Walk to Terezin

The first transport was in November of 1941 but only as far as
Bauschovitz because the Nazis did not hasten the trip till June
one of 1943 after a rail extension direct to Terezin was done.
So those receiving their notice, a bland sinister writing
matter-of-factly stating
that in a very few days from the date on the document
they would be leaving their homes—
they were to restrict their belongings
to a total weighing no more than 110 pounds,
they were to report to a certain location
to be taken by train to the nearest station and then
they must walk the remaining distance over a mile and a half,
no matter the weather, rain or snow or freezing cold,
their new destination must be reached without delay.

This human chain of misery is seen on the dreary day depicted,
surely bedraggled, worn, frazzled
each has summoned from courage or sheer fear the fortitude
to walk on to the place of infamy that lies ahead of them
as the onlookers stare; where are they?
Inside those cozy bungalows which line the vacant sidewalk,
no denizens of this town
whose name will become synonymous with despair
will dare come out from hiding,
so the faces of these houses will stand
as the witnesses to terror:
the windows as eyes open wide, the doors as mouths aghast,
the smoke stacks affecting a Sieg Heil salute
while across the street the trees stand bare,
raising their branches plaintively toward heaven
appealing for those walking by in gloom.
Who endured this walk only to meet their doom?
We cannot know for certain.
Here are names from lists of prisoners: Greta Auerbach,
Arnold Beer, Kamil Cukermandel, Emil Drenger,
Berta Engelmann, Benedikt Fischer, Theresa Gans,
Max Hahn, Samuel Jelinek, Arnostka Karpelesova,
Arnost Lasch, Josef Mayer, Alice Necasova,
Else Olivenova, Wilhelm Pollak, Amalie Reichmann,
Siegfried Schreiber, Jacob Teller, Nathan Ultmann,
Adelheid Vogelova, Louise Weiner, Gustav Ziegler—
May they rest in peace, and may the human race be forgiven.

Names taken from the Central Database of Shoah Victims' Names, of those who perished in Terezin, 1942 or after, Yad Vashem.

Photo from the archive, Jewish Museum in Prague, used with permission

The Train to Terezin

June 1, 1943 — There is no mystery,
It is as clear as the clear day
shown. They, the perpetrators
stand about in wait
for their prey.
A guard stands far away
in the distance seen
high upon the building's roof.
If only he were a witness,
a savior, a chronicler of
evil, what might have been?

Body parts, an arm,
a hand, show out the
open transit camp train windows
yet attached no doubt to
their owners for the time
being until the time comes
and the time will come for
dismembering at Auschwitz and Treblinka.
Who is on the train destined for their demise?
Who knows for sure, here are names from lists of inmates:
Simche Ackermann, Minna Bildstein, Esther Cohen,
Judith Deutsch, Emil Efran, Moses Falkenstein,
Erna Goldschmidt, Gustav Hahn, Franz Jablonsky,
Emil Kahn, Anna Lachmann, Jakob Marcus,
Richard Neumann, Rosa Oppenheimer, Henriette Pessel,
Mendel Rosenbaum, Georg Sass, Klara Thormann,
Isaak Veit, Rosy Wartenberg, Henriette Zamory
May they rest in peace,
and may the human race be forgiven.

Names taken from the Central Database of Shoah Victims' Names, of those who perished in Terezin, 1943 or after, Yad Vashem.

Photo from the archive, Jewish Museum in Prague, used with permission

The Suitcase to Terezin

Josef Ernst is the name on the suitcase.
What can we know from a suitcase?
285 is the number the Nazis assigned to him
for purposes of his transport to Terezin that
day on the train identified as AAw,
and so from lists that were kept
we know he was taken away on the
3rd of August, 1942 from
Horomeritz a quaint Prague village the name
of which appears on the suitcase, his captors
being meticulous about the details of such things
as this and from such records we know Josef Ernst
born 24 June 1900 was liberated from Terezin,
he survived the Holocaust this we know, he had
a life after Terezin and surely now he rests in peace,
we can but hope that he forgave the human race.

Name and information from database of Terezin Initiative nstitute entries for Shoah victims and survivors.

The Tree Of Life

*It is a tree of life for those who hold fast to it,
and all who cling to it find happiness*
—hymn at conclusion of scripture reading portion
of Jewish religious service

He is downtrodden,
disheveled in mind and
spirit, shuffling one foot
in front of the other along
Peldu street in the old
Jewish quarter in Riga
on a rainy October day
searching for where he comes from

a long way from Chicago
where he was born, descended
from umbrella-makers he is told,
he is headed for the soup kitchen
to help serve meals to the elderly.
His life turned upside down;
Parkinson's disease taking its toll.
Why me, why now. Each day he
bargains for a reason like today
his quest for history, he
waits to see what comes his way.
The rain subsides. He turns the
corner. A rainbow appears.
He is consoled.

North Gallery — Nowhere

Sadness In The Midst Of It All

It is just an ordinary day: people going about their everyday affairs, people waiting for a bus or a train, people going in and out of shops, eyeing trinkets, buying a new pair of shoes to replace ones with worn soles, talking together about their day sitting at tables in cafes, just an ordinary day for most but for him, it is misery, sensing catastrophe—the fear of an ending without hope of new beginnings. Living through yet another ensnared by anomie/in the midst of mothers pushing babies in strollers,
children playing and laughing in the streets, just an ordinary day for them, but he might as well be bound in a straitjacket immersed in a glass tank/flooding with water desperately trying to escape before he drowns knowing he is no Houdini disconsolate that the people in the shops, in the cafes, on the bus, do not realize they are privileged to have an ordinary day.

Undercover

Hiding in even the far

reaches of
his mind

guilt, swarming
like locusts in a
biblical verse

preparing for the
Armageddon he

knows is sooner
or later coming

starting with no
intention of
becoming de rigueur

spinning itself
into a coat of
sodden colors over

time

this mantle wearing
upon his every thought

stings as if a poultice
counter to the source
of pain

the shreds,
the torn pieces
of his life

pooling for the discovery.

Michael The Wretch

The ER was bustling when Michael the wretch burst on the scene wreaking havoc when the paramedic asked as is routine what's your social KILL ME FUCK YOU the charge nurse kept trying for any ID at all, combing through computer records frantically searching for a clue, they said they saw his feet sticking out from some bushes at the gas station where they found him drunk, drugged, without food in his belly for at least today, tell us who you are Michael KILL ME FUCK YOU his face so reddened by his panic, the veins of his forehead pulsing, ready to burst, coursing with polluted blood, clenched fists telling the tale of a man possessed by demons, reduced to cursing at the top of his lungs KILL ME FUCK YOU even when they produced the sheets coiled to bind him to the gurney his verbiage remained unrestrained KILL ME FUCK YOU reduced to the persona of a cornered wild animal no humane utterance passed his lips KILL ME FUCK YOU if you only will be nice, then you will be given something to eat KILL ME FUCK YOU moving him finally to a cubicle, the multitude surrounding the spectacle muttering gallows humor, going about their chores having seen this all before, a cadre of doctors and nurses corralled him and a needle found its mark and the beast in him was subdued by barbiturates, his pain extinguished for the briefness of his induced slumber there in an emergency room in the darkest of night with the angel of mercy taking flight as the fight dissipates in his brain burned on acid, devoid of sensibility, his only remaining coded plea
KILL ME FUCK YOU.

Payday Lender Customer Briefly Seen On TV

Good evening, I'm Harriet Ashbury your roving reporter at WNTV and I'm standing here in the middle of this establishment talking to people waiting in line to take out loans against their next paycheck. The new Consumer Financial Protection Bureau has just proposed regulations for these types of short term small loans and we want to find out what those who use these think. So your name is?

Shelly.

Have you been to this place before?

Oh, yes, many times, I'm here to refinance and get $150 now to pay the rent it's due before my next paycheck goes through.

Where do you work?

I'm at Burger Bob's mostly in the back doin' fries.

How much do you earn if you don't mind my asking?

I make eight bucks an hour, they have me work 30 hours, so they don't pay no benefits; my mom, she can't work has a bad back, she takes care of my two little girls so I can be at BB's, so it's hard making it through each week with groceries, rent, you know what I mean.

Where's your husband? Do you have a husband?

He left me, he drank pretty much. It's better he's gone.

Where do you live? Tell me about where you live.

We live at the Acres Inn
just a little ways down the street.

You mean you all live in a motel room?

Yes.

Can't you get assistance, like food stamps,
that sort of thing?

I don't qualify, that's what they told me,
anyway I don't want a hand
out, we make it OK.

Isn't the Acres the place
that just was cited by the Health Department?

Yeah, we got rats, roaches, you try not
to think about it, stay outta their way.

Will you have enough to pay
off the loan when it comes due?

Prob'ly not, it's alright, I'll
roll it over like usual.

But you keep paying
and doesn't the interest just add up?

I don't have no choice, I wanna have
a place for us—we gotta live.

That's all the time we have,
I'm Harriet Ashbury reporting for WNTV, now
back to the newsroom for your local weather.

A Virtual Cry For Help

When I was a younger man
I had a near death experience
by which I mean I nearly died
by the hand of another but
was saved by someone who
then was a brother-in-arms
now a hater, meaning he
loathes me, but yet he saved me
at the time and so since that
time I have been careful to
return the favor meaning
that I take the time to help
my fellow human beings
whenever I can and I came
upon such an occasion an
hour ago in cyberspace.
Just poking through my
Facebook feed I stumbled
upon a post shrieking a
call for help, seeming in despair,
threatening to take her life.

Fortunately I have a
therapist for a daughter
who I turned to in a panic
what could be done I asked
and she answered, calm
and collected and fully
prepared; report this person
needs help. My God, Facebook
is prepared as well, changing my opinion
of this behemoth of social media forever.
Cautioning that this all might
be a prank or just
some poor attention seeking soul,
she gave me words to use
in a comment which I rushed
to post as well, and read that
someone else had written
"forget it folks....she isnt goin
to do dat...bet"
and "go to hell."

The Dead In Me, A Dirge

When I go I want to go suddenly.

They will say he lived 'til the end.

Today the news reports
a 38 year old
zookeeper named Stacey
was killed by a tiger, not
her own species.

Not one of the 1300 statistics
say will be killed today in
this world by someone
who walks upright.

The Ride: Memoriam For Robin Williams

it starts over in a room so dark you cannot see the hand in front

of your face so you want to get out but you cannot see so you think the

only way out is to disappear by killing yourself and then you are

pushed into a tunnel tumbling over and over to an opening

so bright with blinding light radiant beams that you can see even

with your eyes shut tight and you keep spinning inside your head

and you do not know what you just said but you keep on talking instead

of listening to the voice coming from somewhere you do not care where

then it's in your head tingling pumping coursing shaking exhilarating all at

the same time whirling like the dervish you read about in Arabian Nights

but you are not in that exotic place it just feels that way and now you are

dancing in a trance in the middle of a space where sparks are flying

everywhere and it starts over in a room so dark you cannot see the hand

in front of your face so you want to get out but you cannot see so you think

the only way out is to disappear by killing yourself

Visitation

My life has been
wrenched from my
own hands by the horror
of it, I brood constantly
especially at those times of year I say
the prayers of remembrance
for so many murdered souls: my grandparents,
aunts and uncles, cousins all perished
during the Holocaust.
I feel them in my heart,
but have an urging to hear
even just a word from any of
them, all the more to have
the privilege of a question or two
perhaps, with their presence
gracing what would be
such a special moment.

My nephew was
just six during my visit
almost ten years ago,
when I came into his room as
he was talking, so it
appeared, to himself.
He could not say
who was there.

Then just the other day
my own precious little tyke
was found in conversation
with no one in the
living room. A few
weeks went by, when
sorting through a
stack of old photos, while
looking at one of grandpa Samuel,
in whose memory I am named,
my son said, "we talk."

How significant would be at least
some sign for his namesake.

Perhaps it is a matter of merit.
I will work harder.

> *Epigraph:*
> *The unknown sphere, more real than I dreamed,*
> *more direct, darts awakening rays about me*
> *—Walt Whitman, Leaves Of Grass, 1860 ed.*

Prologue:
Turning, staring out the window
the light in the room shows its
reflection in the glass, blades
of light, so the view is a blend
of what's inside and outside
at the same time. What is outside?

A man on a stroll walks by the window
A woman pulling a dog on a leash
two young children running past
it all happened so fast the revolving

red lights spinning around, the sirens
making an awful sound, the police cars
all showing up, the one with the jacket
and tie must be a detective pointing
across the street where the body lie.

Denouement:
Then the girl appeared like a ghost
in white, she opened the door of her toppled car
crawled out and tottered over to the officers in blue who
waved at her with hard fists, and other officers,
as the crowd gathered, motioning them away
the crime scene tape macabrely festooned
the roadway from side to side where
skid marks tellingly showed the braking and the speed.

The mother of the child on the ground cried.
It was a sad scene, an awakening, far too late.

Epilogue:
The Buddhists have an awakening in their view,
the way to the end of suffering, achieved
by overturning false belief, not a vehicle
would that the tragedy witnessed itself be false not true,
follow the Eightfold Path to Nirvana it is urged, but
surely the path leads not down this highway.

Sliver Of A Moon

Like an opening
of small proportions,
just sufficing
to signify there is
a shimmer of light
out there in the ether
in the darkness of the
night sky to show
there remains even at
its nadir a slender
hope out there
somewhere.

South Gallery — Somewhere

A More Perfect Union: Excerpts From A Summer Journal*

(Reading a book in which appear Lincoln's words given at Gettysburg. That the new nation was brought forth and dedicated to the proposition that all are created equal. He said: "we can not dedicate we can not consecrate we can not hallow" those who struggled here have.)

Charleston, June 28th
Arrived on Friday
with church bells
ringing for Carolina Day
sponsored by the
Palmetto Society
first celebrated in 1777
they say to a year and
six days removed from
the Declaration.
The guide, Miss Sara, in her
long cotton dress, a true
southern belle. Her auburn
hair tied up inside her wide brimmed
hat with its yellow ribbon trailing
behind sitting in wicker
on the veranda
of the plantation house
drinking sweet tea
a concoction laden with
enough sugar to ensure no
bitter taste from a bygone era.
Walked Slave Street,
euphemistically named compared to
the row of nine original ramshackle
brick shanties where lived in squalor
the great house servants.
Later the United Daughters
of the Confederacy will participate
in a wreath-laying ceremony at
White Point Gardens honoring
the fallen from a fateful day in not
the Civil but Revolutionary War.

New York, July 22nd
Arrived on Saturday.
Across from the hotel
in Manhattan workers are loading
a big red van with the mover's
name Moishe's Worldwide
Moving emblazoned proudly on the
side in billboard-size white
letters for all the world to see.
The message on hotel stationery
lay on the nightstand in the room:
From Concierge, Vladimir – I was
informed that the majority of the
shops on Orchard Street will be
open on Sunday.
The Lower East Side: A.W. Kaufman
Lingerie; Ziontalis, Judaica
Department Store

since 1920; Kadouri
Import, Israeli produce;
Gertel's Bakery; and there at
97 Orchard Street,
as mentioned in the guidebook,
The Tenement Museum.
The docent was of Italian descent,
with thick Brooklyn accent, and black
olive eyes. He told of his ancestors
as so many now
inscribed on the Wall Of Honor erected
there, enduring steerage,
and the gauntlet of
the gateway, Ellis Island.
He told of Nathalie Gumpertz,
a German Jewish
seamstress, in 1874 she became
the sole support of her
four young children after
her husband disappeared.
He told of the hunger, the sweatshops,
the firebrand labor organizers,
rabble-rousers some say,
they took to the street,
many were struck down but they won
hard fought victories on
that battleground.

Washington D.C., August 30th
Arrived on Sunday.
Staying in Georgetown.
It is all very quaint. Walked along the
towpath of the Chesapeake
and Ohio Canal, like
much before and since
the water highway no longer
the new way
replaced by the rise of the railway.
Visited the National Gallery of Art,
saw the American Collection,
The White House, the Washington
Monument. There adjacent to
the National Mall,
stands the United States
Holocaust Memorial Museum.
Somber faced people go in
and come out chastened.
Identification Cards given
at the entrance tell
the stories of victims;
on each cover
the statement,
apt for all time, "For the dead
and the living we must bear witness."
Across from the Lincoln
Memorial is the Vietnam
Veterans Memorial,
a long, slow-rising
wall bearing the names
of almost 60,000
Americans who died or
remain missing.
It is all chronological,
from the first listed
casualty in 1959 to
the last in 1975.
The visitors' grim faces
reflect in the shiny
black granite. Many
look for their loved ones' names—
summer days end amid such sad
searches urging in pleas
unvoiced for a more
perfect Union.

*in homage to Pete Seeger (1919-2014)

From Generation To Generation

"Just think about it, a blizzard this time of year. I can't understand it! But I see the handwriting on the wall. We're not going anywhere any time soon."

"What writing on what wall? What do you mean? First time flying? These things happen, mister, so you need to chill, take out your MP3 player or whatever, and make the best of it. Where are you going, anyway?"

"What's an MP3 player? And yes, after bein' around ninety-two years this past spring, it's my first time flyin'—if I make it on the plane. I have a sick brother in Toledo."

"Sorry about your brother. Here, listen. This plays all my music. I don't suppose you know what rap is, do you? Oops, sorry, that's my phone. I gotta take this call. Hi, dad. I'm still at the airport in Minneapolis. You got the letter? Go ahead, read it to me . . . Oh no! Give me a few minutes, I'll call back."

"You look like you've seen a ghost. What's wrong?"

"They turned me down. I just heard from the grad school I wanted. I didn't make it."

"Look, it's none of my business, but you can't let a setback get to you. When I was your age, I went into dry cleaning in Red Wing. I borrowed the money, then my partner cleaned me out, if you get me, and disappeared. You just got to pick yourself up and start over. You know what they say, if at first you don't succeed, try, try again."

"My grandad used to say that. Thanks for the advice. Hey, can I take your picture?"

"Sure you can, but you don't have a camera."

"My smartphone has a camera. They all do, you know."

"In my day you didn't walk around with a phone in your pocket, or read a book on a TV screen you hold in your hand like that girl over there showed me. We had real books, encyclopedias on the shelf. How do you even find out things nowadays?"

"It's pretty much all online."

"Online you say. That's why I don't have a ticket. They said I shoulda gone online for that. Bet they won't let me on. It don't matter anyhow because the way things are going, I'll probably meet my maker before we ever get out of here!"

I Don't Look Up At The Sky Anymore

When I was growing up,
we lived in the boonies, the
edge of civilization where J.C.
lost his shoes some said;
eventually it all became just
another part of the amalgam
that is metro Chicago,
grown as if from vines, each
intertwines with the rooted heart of town
so when you drive around on a street
you know it just seems now
only stoplights signal
the change from place to place;
but back then we were pioneers
living on subverted farmland sold
for a pot of gold to developers who
promised paradise to those who made
the trek to trade the advertised woes of city life
for celebrated suburban tranquility.

So in the early evening, if the weather
was right, and the mosquitoes weren't
ready to bite, I wandered out to the backyard
and lay down in the grass, which I may
have mowed earlier in the day
and because we were a ways a way
from the city lights, the sky lit up with
stars, and the fireflies were there as well
and you almost couldn't tell which was which
with so many of each in sight
and the new-mown grass smell
was sweet and lying there
I felt anything was possible.

Dear Daughter Mine

I know you now live near Washington, D.C. far away

from me. I know we keep in touch with phone texts and such

sharing on Facebook virtually. I'm really writing to say

we had a great time, mom and I, when you spent

a few days with your husband and

the twins who had their seventh birthday just a while back

yet seem so much older now than when last you came.

I asked them what they liked best, having left here

where they were born, for a more northern clime.

They answered that after it snows and they go sledding

mommy makes hot cocoa. Anyway, the weather

here in Florida is not like there of course this time of year,

you've had your first taste of winter that's for sure.

I know you thought that part of visiting

was fine even on the very breezy day

we all went to the beach to play in the sand,

to squish our toes and feet in the ocean's

foaming surf, the water aquamarine

like Key West you said, the most

special thing was flying those kites;

I Don't Look Up At The Sky Anymore

When I was growing up,
we lived in the boonies, the
edge of civilization where J.C.
lost his shoes some said;
eventually it all became just
another part of the amalgam
that is metro Chicago,
grown as if from vines, each
intertwines with the rooted heart of town
so when you drive around on a street
you know it just seems now
only stoplights signal
the change from place to place;
but back then we were pioneers
living on subverted farmland sold
for a pot of gold to developers who
promised paradise to those who made
the trek to trade the advertised woes of city life
for celebrated suburban tranquility.

So in the early evening, if the weather
was right, and the mosquitoes weren't
ready to bite, I wandered out to the backyard
and lay down in the grass, which I may
have mowed earlier in the day
and because we were a ways a way
from the city lights, the sky lit up with
stars, and the fireflies were there as well
and you almost couldn't tell which was which
with so many of each in sight
and the new-mown grass smell
was sweet and lying there
I felt anything was possible.

Dear Daughter Mine

I know you now live near Washington, D.C. far away

from me. I know we keep in touch with phone texts and such

sharing on Facebook virtually. I'm really writing to say

we had a great time, mom and I, when you spent

a few days with your husband and

the twins who had their seventh birthday just a while back

yet seem so much older now than when last you came.

I asked them what they liked best, having left here

where they were born, for a more northern clime.

They answered that after it snows and they go sledding

mommy makes hot cocoa. Anyway, the weather

here in Florida is not like there of course this time of year,

you've had your first taste of winter that's for sure.

I know you thought that part of visiting

was fine even on the very breezy day

we all went to the beach to play in the sand,

to squish our toes and feet in the ocean's

foaming surf, the water aquamarine

like Key West you said, the most

special thing was flying those kites;

first time for the kids, what a sight, they holding
the lines so tight, the flapping flimsy frames
taking the torment of the swirling seaside winds
the news said 20 miles an hour with gusts of more.
So we triumphed there to say the least and I became
grandpa hero once again. Our hootenanny
was lots of fun. One playing a slide whistle the other
the kazoo dancing and prancing around while
I plucked out a banjo tune to Five Foot Two
and Muffin Man before the big finale surprising mom
with Burl Ives' Big Rock Candy Mountain which her
father sang to her when she was young.
I never learned the song before that night,
It was like my gift to her, I hope she thought so too.
Then the morning that you left, heading back to life
from nine to five, I clicked the PBS website and played
Mr. Rodgers' You Are Special for the twins; they never
heard it before if you didn't know so I gave them
copies to practice for our next big show and
I'm really writing to say: "If there ever comes a day
when we can't be together keep me in your heart, I'll stay
there forever" which is a quote from Winnie the Pooh, love you, dad.

The author "having his fill" after a hard day on the road, c.1958

On The Road To Matrimony

The escapade had its just desserts, as I met my wife of now 50 years on account of it. Back in 1958 when I was just 15, dear old dad, in the automobile biz himself at the time, slipped someone downtown a little incentive in return for a driver's license with my name on it a year before its time. Compounding the "felony" he rewarded me with a dilapidated brown Dodge sedan, rust spots to match, but rust or not that car put me ahead of the pack.

I was attracted to her right off the bat when first we met at a dance on the Northwest Side in Chicago; to get there, I drove petrified through city traffic from way out in the sticks where I lived. The next day I went to pick her up, met her folks; they let me take her for a drive. On the way back we stopped at Amy Joy Donuts for a baker's dozen. Sitting in her kitchen, I ate 12, she had one. I was in love.

The New Cat

Our old cat died in '98.
She lived some 20 years
in the house in which our
daughters grew to womanhood.
She left us a month after
my father-in-law died, hearts
gave out for both.
The girls used to put her
in a doll carriage, tied
a bonnet on her head
she let them do that.
It took me all this time
to learn to live with the
fact she was no more.
She's laid to rest in
the backyard, underneath
a stone birdbath, she would
have liked that I think.
We have a new cat now,
Tiger is his name.
He came our way
just days before
we got the news
my brother-in-law
had died of cancer.
Somebody said at
the funeral, dying
is a part of living.
Which, the easy
or the hard part?

Growing Up With M&M's

M&M's came along in 1941.
I came along in 1943.
We've spent a long time
together since

the time of World War II
over in Guam my father
got the news two years

after I was born
he first heard from me
on an old '78
sound booth recording
of my mother's voice
and mine too cooing
I loved him though
I'd never met him

I remember
when he came
home,
together we'd
wash my trike,
he'd wash the
cab he drove to

pay the bills
to buy the
clothes, the milk
the M&M's he
got me for a treat

to me, M&M's are more
than something to eat.

Learning Right From Wrong

by a species of fine frenzy - an ecstatic intuition –
—Edgar Allan Poe, "The Philosophy of Composition"

Today was Free Comic Book Day throughout the U.S.A. I have to tell you all about this major momentous mega-event from the standpoint of the two under-aged participants accompanying me on this excursion into the pages of *Howard Lovecraft and the Frozen Kingdom/The Unknowns* a rock band who are secretly alien cops, *Camp Midnight* A human female mistakenly sent to a summer camp for monsters, *Junior Braves of the Apocalypse* in which a troupe of boys returns from a camping trip to find the zombie apocalypse in full effect. *Captain America* is there, *The Phantom* too, plus *Valiant 2016*, brooding, dark, gothic transformations from the everyday to metahuman worlds akin to nevermore. So off we trod to find our destination Past Present Future Comic Superstore wherein we encountered immediately upon entering a panoply the likes of which could not be imagined except in dreams: there before us stood Spiderman, Catwoman, a stormtrooper, Deadpool, but to name a few, all willing to take our side and be our guide through this unaccustomed ride in a place where the hubbub resembled the Cantina scene from Star Wars Episode IV, and the people too, decked out in freakish style, one of my own compatriots sporting hair of blue.

Can this be true I mused as I was handed a plastic bag of no less than five fantastic journeys in glossy print my choices in keeping with the farthest reaches of my imagination beyond the grasp of the paltry reality I live from day to day. I said to myself, Who is to say we can not get away

at least to play the way
we entertained
when we were wee. The
younglings I was with were
totally enthralled venturing
out into the bright
sun of day from our flight
into the emergent seeming
night alike to nevermore.

It was during a brief repast
as respite that the idea
came to mind, not mine,
of one who had not yet
reached the time of maturity,
when the possible is
understood, perhaps we
might take another bite
from some unsuspecting sister
store, a mammoth score!
So the debate ensued among
us three, two being not much
over four feet tall. I argued
it was not fair, we had our share.
The consensus was otherwise,

as a mutiny gives rise to
dangerous decisions. Our
connivance was to be discrete,
and so when we had our fill
to eat we plied our trade
across the street at Tate's
Comics Toys and More.
Triumph was to be our destiny
as we stood in line yet
once again, this time
rewarded with four more
fantasy creations fit for
our other appetite. Were
we right, I thought, considering
the matter. Next month is
Supercon, a veritable
feast with vendors galore,
of Comic Book,
Anime, and other such reverie.
Will the plot be played
out once again,
or nevermore?

Blessed Union

What is there to say after close to 50 years of marriage?
We met at 15 though the finagled driver's license I had said
I was older hoping to impress the girls with the Dodge sedan
I sported, the brown color hiding the rust spots, but rust or not,
I figured it put me ahead of the pack. It was love at first sight.
Not a silver screen attraction but something else. I didn't know
about soul mates back then; it was fate, kismet, a destined future
that drew us together at a dance in a place on the Northwest side
of Chicago called Peterson Park. Actually it was Susan somebody
who found my sweaty palms off-putting and pushed together
the future mister and missus. The next day I took her to an
ice cream parlor that no longer exists. The wedding was at
the old Villa Venice, complete with Venetian canal and gondolas.
The place burned down right after, maybe razed for the insurance,
so that's gone now too. When she was pregnant with our first
daughter she broke her leg in a freak accident with another
junk of a car, a Buick I think with an aluminum engine
that never started in cold weather. It wasn't easy getting
around nine months pregnant in a cast. We moved to Upstate
New York where it seemed always to be cold, so we traded
the Buick for a red Datsun wagon. Then a second
baby girl came along and life started lurching forward.
The company I worked for folded. I scrambled to find another
job, to put food on the table, to pay the bills. I'm not saying we
didn't have good times along the way, but I can't stop thinking
about the heart attacks, the scraping by, the literally
crazy family members that caused us anguish and grief.
What do we have after almost 50 years?

A mortgage that will never be paid for in our lifetime,
photos of the cars that died, and loved ones that died.
A year ago she had a stroke. The doctor said go on with
your life. But when she gets a headache, I worry, when
she is out of sight I go to check that she's alright.
We have each other, that's true, in the morning to wake up
next to, to sit with, while reading the headlines at breakfast,
while riding in our aging—so are we—Toyota.
Getting out of our car we hold hands, still she takes my hand
even with my sweaty palms. We walk up to the door of our
younger daughter's house. Ringing the bell we hear two excited tikes,
the grandkids, giggling with glee. She looks at me, there's no place
we'd rather be. For the time we have left, in sickness and in health,
for better or for worse, in good times and bad, for richer or poorer,
crying together or laughing together, stuck on the highway with a flat,
in fear of the knock at the door, the letter in the mail
like the power of Niagara Falls—the common man's
honeymoon haunt—life's hurts and hazards,
pits and prongs, can never match the magnitude
of love that is two as one. It's a blessed union.

My Friend Is Leaving *

He is going away;
while we wait,
he is lying in a bed
in a hospital
hospice wing
barely hearing
my plea
go peacefully.
Death, the
other side of living—
watching dying trying
to reconcile
the vibrant life
you led with the
way I see you now
I remember memories:
the drive down to
Coconut Grove, our annual
trek to the art fair down there
all the time on the way
debating some inane point of
politics yours right mine left;
your finding the singer Eva Cassidy
who also left too soon—
melanoma as I recall, her
Over The Rainbow
reinvented the original, the final
cut on her album Songbird,
you gave me that;
you showed me the value
of tenacity of purpose
from our early days together,
you helped me understand
the merit of the good fight
and the stories that you told
of the characters in your
past kept me laughing
will keep me laughing.
A particular favorite in my mind,
has me smiling even now.
You are on your way, out
of time, out of strength
you have bravely borne
an anguished later life
no one deserves
the last few years
you were dealt
you had your run
to say the least
but I saw your tears
well up the last
visit you were sitting up
and we talked like in times
before, as friends do.
Your wife gave my wife
an embroidered pillow
some time back
on which is written
"It takes a long time
to grow an old friend"
Indeed, and then it is forever.

in homage to G. Samwick (1939 - 2014)

Unscathed

I am near four score if granted vigor.
Who is dead today? The counting
continues after Ecuador's earthquake.
587 as of now. I sat next to a woman
in a meeting at 10 a.m. and learned her
grandson of 17 had taken a street drug
that caused his premature demise.
Who is dead today?
The 6 o'clock news reports about a
motorcyclist who lost control
of his bike, smashed through
a guardrail and took a spill into
a ravine, he did not survive; stage 4 cancer
ended the life of a 35 year old down
the block, her husband and two young
children now have neither wife
nor mother; the obituaries
in today's paper fill 3 pages,
with those listed from infancy to what
some call comfortable old age,
not to mention the deaths mete
out by malevolence. Who is
dead today? Celebrities like Prince,
and recently too Doris Roberts,
Merle Haggard, Patty Duke,
Garry Shandling, Frank Sinatra Jr.
just to name a few,
yet for some reason
unknown, yet for
some purpose to unfold,
yet there are those
who stand unscathed, like me.

The old photograph depicts my father, my grandfather, my brother, and me at the Museum of Science and Industry in Chicago. It's from the Street of Yesteryear exhibit. We're sitting in an old Model T, my brother probably 7 at the time, mock-steering behind the wheel. The exhibit has existed ever since I can recall, it is always as it was before, no matter how long you've been gone. It stands the test of time. Like the pyramids. So I was sure to take my wife and daughters there to have our picture taken in the same photogravure studio, next to the Nickelodeon still showing Perils of Pauline two reelers ad infinitum to the evocative accompaniment of a piano just as if it were 1915. It's become family tradition, this picture taking pilgrimage. My eldest daughter on a visit to our hometown several years ago brought her husband and two children, my grandchildren, to that very place to ensure the next generation is encapsulated by the 11x14 Century Portrait camera which stands at the ready for every such occasion. So when I took a look the other day imagine my dismay to see my grandfather literally fading away. I am resolute to find a means to save him. I owe him that. He pictured *the way*.

Sunrise On Big Pine Key Revisited

I woke that morning saying to myself
why am I here? Just the day before
I was packing, cajoled into
a trip to the Keys by friends who
meant well. "It'll do you good" one
of them said, knowing what I was
going through. We all chipped in,
rented a beach house, planned to
spend New Year's there, basking
in the sun, frolicking in the ocean.
I didn't feel much like having fun.
"I'm being hijacked" I said
only half kidding as we piled
into the van. Our route began in
West Palm Beach; a five hour
drive to most anywhere is a drudge,
but not so I'll admit heading to the Keys.

Coming down U.S. Route One
you become the pilot of what
surely seems an amphibious
vehicle steeped in the aquamarine
of the Overseas Highway where
the Gulf meets the Atlantic.

I stood by the sea
consumed with perplexity.
thinking about my
daughter's infertility,
my father's Parkinson's,
my brother's heart attack.
Why would someone so
loving be deprived, why
would someone so strong
be brought low, why would
someone so full of life be stilled?

There I stood, by the ocean's edge
witnessing the sun rising
seemingly right out of the water.

There I watched as billowing clouds swirled around
an azure sky meeting the ocean
in a cascade of hues of blue

There I immersed myself in the surf at dawn
amid the roar of sound pounding
around my ankles and my feet.

I slept that night wrapped in such thoughts
and the morning I spent on
the sand at the shore.

Running Out Of Gas

The old gas pump
stands well used
and rusted
outside the 50's diner
seen by most as
just a relic on display
along a stretch of
US Highway One
a long way
from Springfield, Mass.
the place it still calls home.

Back in its heyday
it was something special.
Bright, shiny, and new.

Full of spunk. Ready to go.
Waiting to serve.

Now, when you
squeeze the handle
it creaks and shudders
into a semi-wakeful
state as if to say
I'm here, I'm trying
give me a chance.

But its numbers still count.

Morning Blessings

I am awake, a blessing,
I see the blazing sun
rising in the morning's
bluish sky, a blessing,
I walk to the kitchen smelling
the fragrance of limes
wafting on an incoming
breeze arriving at my window, a blessing.
I pour my steaming coffee, cradling my cup
in weathered yet still agile hands, a blessing,
I read the paper retrieved
from my doorstep, debating in my mind
the stories of the day,
a blessing. The phone rings,
I answer, speaking my hello
to someone I know and love, a blessing;
I go outside, and kneel before a stand
of purple morning-glories, a few I take
to grace my breakfast table, a blessing.
From the cupboard I remove my usual fare,
it being there, a blessing. The carpenter
arrives to repair wood rotted on the porch
and when he's done I pay him for his
fix, the money available for this, a blessing.
I hear the barking of the dog next store
the chirping of a bird flying in from unknown
climes to greet my day, a blessing.
I notice out my window, children playing
in the street, a blessing, mothers pushing
babies in strollers, a blessing, my neighbor's son
banging on his drum, a blessing
writing down these words, a blessing.

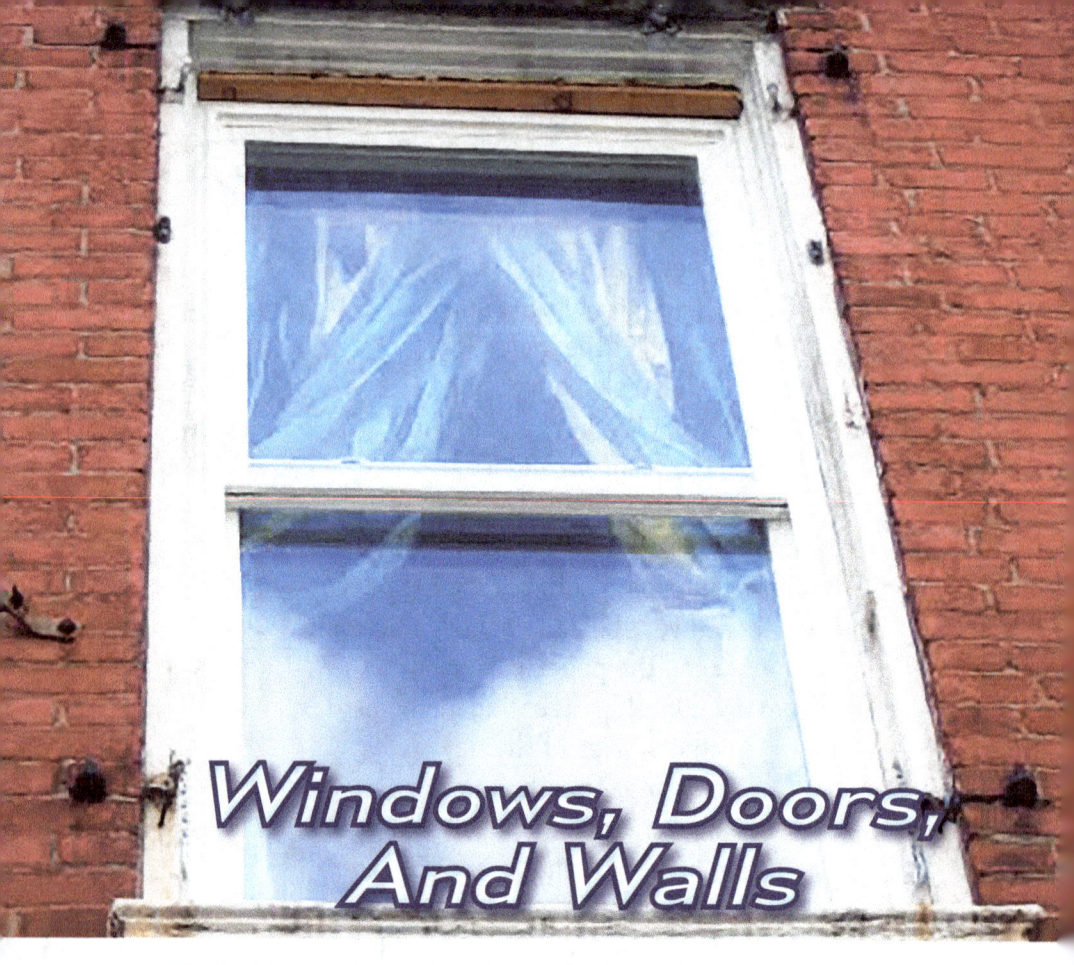

Windows, Doors, And Walls

Here looking out the window, drawing back the drapery
to see through the pane, depending on the day,
squinting to view the dazzling light of a new morning
or seeing rain pouring down on the street below.
Sometimes it starts with rain, the day I think about
staring out the window, will I find myself today?
I can stay at the window or go to the door.

The door is closed until I open it and walk
out onto the sidewalk, bright with sunlight or

wet beneath my feet from the early
morning rain. I stand and scan
all that surrounds
me as I seize the day,
searching for a sign within the
compass of my shadow

on the pavement very far
from a place I can call home.

The walls I encounter walking on my way,
they are all around to make me stop
and wonder where next to go while still
seeking a telling sign, the walls
change my course, shift my direction.

Along the way doors open to new worlds within
should I enter upon such invitations—

and other doors lead to nowhere
and if I dare turn

toward a route that
takes me to what
appears ahead
I will find myself
in a place beyond
where I am *here* now
and given time, I will
meander amid the
windows, doors, and walls

there in a place
I can call home.

Pictured here, as well as on the back cover, the author at Bowne & Co., 19th Century job printer's shop, South Street Seaport, New York; pioneer printing concern founded in 1775

About me

My work was first published later in life, at age 70, to be exact; I had won a poetry prize way back when, which should have been encouraging, but I had other fish to fry. I married, started a family, took up marketing communications and advertising — *copywriting is writing*, I said to myself. I also had ambitions as a young man to write songs. I haunted some of the same coffee houses where a fellow named Deutschendorf plied his trade, aka John Denver. At some point, I even sent a demo tape to Nashville. Never heard back. I kept on the working man's track. No regrets. Then the muse started gnawing at me, I started writing again. Graves said "There's no money in poetry, but then there's no poetry in money, either." It has paid off, not in coin of the realm, but rather in finding that my creative endeavors have moved people, have sounded at least a few virtual chords. It has been said poetry is the music of language. If so, I *do* write songs. A recurring theme in my work is that enunciated in the thought of Mexican artist Frida Kahlo (1907 - 1954): "At the end of the day, we can endure much more than we think we can." My interest in this theme in general is sparked by the work of Elisabeth Kübler-Ross (1926 – 2004). She had this to say on the subject: "The most beautiful people we have known are those who have known defeat, known suffering, known struggle, known loss, and have found their way out of the depths."

Howard Richard Debs received a University of Colorado Poetry Prize at age 19. After spending the past fifty years in the field of communications, with recognitions including a Distinguished Achievement Award from the Educational Press Association of America, he resumed his creative pursuits. Finalist and recipient 28th Annual 2015 Anna Davidson Rosenberg Poetry Awards, his work appears internationally in numerous publications such as Yellow Chair Review, Silver Birch Press, China Grove, The Galway Review, Cleaver Magazine, the Clear Poetry 2015 Anthology, among others. His photography will be found in select publications, including in Rattle online as "Ekphrastic Challenge" artist and guest editor.

www.ingramcontent.com/pod-product-compliance
Lightning Source LLC
Chambersburg PA
CBHW052122070526
44586CB00016B/2038